POETICA 9

The Golden Apple

Elen
Belen
Balbadelen
Corn
Horn
Jig
Golden fig
Chipple chapple
Golden Apple
Away with it

The Golden Apple

*A Round
of stories, songs, spells,
proverbs and riddles*

chosen and translated by
Andrew Harvey and Anne Pennington

from
Od Zlata Jabuka
compiled by

VASKO POPA

ANVIL PRESS POETRY

This revised edition published in 2010
by Anvil Press Poetry Ltd
Neptune House 70 Royal Hill London SE10 8RF
www.anvilpresspoetry.com
First published in hardback in 1980

ISBN 978 0 85646 419 5

This book is published
with financial assistance from
Arts Council England

A catalogue record for this book
is available from the British Library

Designed and set in Monotype Fournier by Anvil
Printed and bound in Great Britain
by Hobbs the Printers Ltd

CONTENTS

INTRODUCTION

THIS book was not intended by its compiler, Vasko Popa, to be a comprehensive anthology of Serbo-Croatian folk literature – a representative selection of the many different genres – but rather a "garland" (we have called it a "round") of compositions chosen for their poetic merit by a contemporary poet. In a postscript Popa explains that his choice was never influenced by received opinion as to which compositions should be accounted poetry and which not; he followed only his own poetic taste, collecting pieces that he himself loved, and finding "great joy in bringing the little-known and under-valued beauties of old riddles, proverbs, spells, curses and counting rhymes out of the shadows into daylight." The translators have inevitably narrowed the selection still further by following the same principles: we kept only those compositions whose poetic qualities could survive translation.

Popa arranged the compositions as a number of cycles, each cycle containing one text, or group of texts, of each genre, loosely linked by theme. By this Popa ensures that proverbs and riddles illuminate and echo each other vividly, without need for the explanations that one finds in traditional anthologies where items are arranged alphabetically. We have kept as far as possible the same arrangement, although our omissions have entailed certain alterations.

The anthologies from which Popa took these compositions are listed at the back of the book. He took them more or less as he found them, abbreviating only some of the longer stories, to keep "the most poetic part". He simplified the titles of the spells, but kept the titles of stories and songs; where there was none he used the first line as title. The titles of the riddles are their answers. By this Popa aims at "re-establishing for the reader the natural movement of the creative process".

In translating we have kept as closely as possible to the original. The stories, riddles, proverbs, even the spells, usually seemed to come easily into English. The songs (or poems – the Serbo-Croat word covers both meanings) present more problems. In the Serbo-Croat folk tradition songs are divided into heroic and "women's" songs. The heroic songs are mostly sung by men, accompanied by the one-string fiddle (the *gusle*), are directed at an audience, and tell a story; the women's songs are lyrical, are sung predominantly (though not exclusively) by women, and are often associated with particular occasions (such as weddings, harvest). They are usually unaccompanied and are sung by the singers for themselves and not for an audience. The songs in this book are lyrical songs: Popa excluded heroic songs from his anthology because as he said "they are organic parts of a rounded whole, hewn out of marble, which cannot, which must not, be cut in pieces."

Formally these lyrical songs are extremely varied; a few have stanza form, many follow the regular decasyllabic line also used in the heroic songs. Rhyming is irregular, but great use is made of alliteration, especially in pleonastic phrases and in fixed epithets; the declensional and conjugational system of Serbo-Croat also makes partial rhyming at the end of the line natural. Popa has chosen some songs with refrains, although he has made our task easier by largely excluding senseless jingles. Parallel or antithetical constructions, very characteristic of South and East Slavonic singing, are often used in these songs: we have retained them as often as possible. We have not followed exactly all the repetitions, nor have we attempted to find a similar syllabic or rhyming structure in English. We have tried to keep the atmosphere and spirit of the original and so have aimed at making vivid and immediate English poems.

Folk literature played a crucial role in the development of the modern Serbo-Croatian literary language. The first codifier of the language, Vuk Stefanović Karadžić (1787–1862), was also the first great compiler of folk-literature anthologies – Popa's principal source for this collection. Vuk lived much of his life in Vienna and was profoundly influenced by the Romantic celebration of the "natural man", that is, the peasant. Vuk rejected the artificial hybrid language, Russo-Slavonic, which was used in Serbia for works with literary pretensions, and based his grammar (1814) and his dictionary (1818) firmly on popular usage. He included copious illustrative material from folk-literature, drawing on the immense collections of songs, stories and sayings which he himself made. Folk compositions had not previously been appreciated in literary circles in Serbia, but gradually, owing partly to the acclaim of foreign writers – Goethe, Jacob Grimm, Sir Walter Scott were among them – Vuk's "popular" language was accepted in Serbia.

Vuk collected his material from a wide geographical area, from Montenegro, Dalmatia, Bosnia, Croatia, as well as from Serbia proper: although distinguished by accent and vocabulary, the dialects of all these areas show very similar grammatical features and are mutually comprehensible (far more so than the dialects of German or of English). Vuk's linguistic work found a parallel in Croatia in that of the so-called Illyrian Movement, led by Ljudevit Gaj, which was fighting for the use of the popular language rather than the Latin, Hungarian and German which were the literary languages of the Croatian area. Gaj's reform and Vuk's agreed to such an extent that in 1850 it was possible for Serbian and Croatian writers to sign a Literary Agreement ("Književni Dogovor") in Vienna, which formally brought into existence a single literary language – modern Serbo-Croatian – a language firmly rooted in popular usage.

Writers in Serbo-Croat, then, can have an unusually creative relationship with folk literature. Vasko Popa has shown in his own writing the "winged steps" that can be taken by writing out of the folk literary tradition, "the poetic foundation of our language." Here, in *The Golden Apple*, we see some of the magic and pagan elements which have intrigued readers of Popa – the disembodied hands and heads, witches stealing live hearts, the stars of heaven mirrored by the sheep on the field. We see some of the games and curses which he wove into the powerful cycles of *Unrest-Field*. The freshness of approach in riddles is used by Popa to bring "sleeping idioms" to life: for instance, time conventionally "flows" in Serbo-Croat, but when St Sava with time flowing to his left and right "strides on dry land" the image is refreshed. Even the folk poet's fixed epithet has its counterpart in the recurring words and symbols of Popa – the most obvious example being the wolf, which roams from book to book. In more general ways also Popa is indebted to the folk tradition: his poetry has a sensuous immediacy, wit, and detached hard radiance that is the reward of a long and deep involvement with it. As Popa has written in his preface to *The Golden Apple*, "the one, true, untarnishable tradition of folk poetry is constant invention, constant discovery."

Popa's bold and skilled inventiveness makes him an ideal guide to the poetic riches of the Serbo-Croatian folk tradition; it is our hope that this collection from his *Golden Apple* will give the English reader some idea of that tradition's power and range and beauty.

ANDREW HARVEY
ANNE PENNINGTON
1980

PREFACE

Just before midnight, he woke up and looked at the tree. It was just beginning to ripen, the whole courtyard shone with it.

('The Golden Apple and the Nine Peahens')

The shepherd went through the wood, and as he went he heard and understood all that the birds and the grass and everything else in the world was saying.

('The Animals' Language')

OUR FOLK POETRY flowered and fruited deep in the heart of hundred-year nights. In this dark age, our literature's golden age took shape. Our one true classical heritage. An age of epic, song and story, whose miraculous beauty shines from inconceivably far away, shedding its eternal light on all poetic creations which rise on this griddle of earth beneath this sky.

The folk bard still seems at one with the natural world around him, still hears the flowers grow, the chick hatch from the egg, the stars spawn. In his song the earth and sun open their hearts and speak forth in human speech. His rhythms express the dance of the sun's rays, the winds and the branches. Through his eyes, stone and wood gain the gift of sight, attaining a stature known only to man, to a bard.

This universal dimension, which measures and shapes every-thing our people's poems sing of and hold, from human to ant to star, lends its language a witching charm that no generation can resist. This, the presence of the whole universe in every thing, is why folk poetry and song is the template from which the world was created – or, more precisely, a template which one might use to create a world to live in. To live in following humankind's only wish: humanly, humanely. In these poems we glimpse that world's glittering archetypes, fabulous and unrepeatable.

The folk bard does not show his loyalty to nature (which gives him life and takes it away) by blindly imitating what nature has created, but by applying nature's creative act to what he wishes to create. And that act of creation is obstinate, unexpected, inexplicable. Its fruits are the golden apples of story on the forking tree of human invention. And in so doing and being, the bard passes on this one priceless message to his future fellows: those impassioned with the same task of extending and enriching this world with words of song. Yet nowhere does this poetic act manifest itself as purely, in all its reckless, crazy beauty, as in the creations of this first poet.

This too is why our greatest poets, from decade to decade, from century to century, return to the eternally living wellspring of folk poetry. There, deep in the poetic soil of our mother tongue (which no poem can leap free of, however winged), all too often buried beneath the moss and sand of forgetting, bubbles the source of all our surging poetic currents past and to come. But one cannot scoop the living water from these springs by retracing the beaten track of fashionable faux-ethnic traditionalism. The one, true, untarnishable tradition of folk poetry is constant invention, constant discovery. Tradition's undimmable flame lights only the way ahead: one has to hew one's own new track through the living rock of one's own age. And those who walk this rugged road risk both death and eternal life.

Today, the voices of a new Generation are making themselves heard all over the globe, first faintly, then loud and clear – a Generation which, this time, seeks to build on the rediscovered foundations and pillars of popular art. In this we can only pride ourselves on the poetic wealth of our own people: now we do not need to roam the world, because this wealth makes us one with the whole world. Staring deep into the mirrors of our folk poetry, into the dizzying whirlpool from which that poetry springs, beneath the surface of each word we seem to glimpse the magic keys which open the secret gates of beauty – the beauty which man makes in order to conquer ugliness, time and death.

We listen to the never-ending song of the folk bard, our own word's first father and son, its first master and servant, we listen to his song and hear, hidden in its flesh, our ancient jugular vein coursing from tradition to tradition, now ringing like a nightingale, now roaring like a storm, until it reaches the one our poets are waiting to fashion and pass on to tomorrow. By tracking the course of that fecund underground river, which keeps its ultimate secrets concealed from the light of day, we can penetrate into the world's innermost heart, and only then can we make even a single beat of that heart heard in the voice of our land and people. We must not lose sight, even for an instant, of this vein which brings us our lifeblood; we must not let it be cut. Whenever it is cut, whenever it dries, our singing branches are silenced, the present slams its head against a wall, and we must bid all futures farewell.

We chant and tell ourselves these songs, riddles, proverbs, spells, curses and tales born in time out of mind, and they rise before us in new, undreamt-of splendour, fresh and untapped as if they had appeared today. And they will do so still, as long as sun and earth and the magic of our mother tongue remain. As long as we keep repeating our love, forever new and forever true to the poems and songs of our people.

Vasko Popa

1966

Translated by Francis R. Jones

NOTE ON PRONUNCIATION

Proper names have been transliterated according to accepted Serbo-Croatian practice. The following points may be noted:

c is pronounced like *ts* in *fits*
č is pronounced like *ch* in *cheese*
ć is a softer version of *č*
đ is pronounced like *j* in *juice*
h is pronounced like *ch* in Scottish *loch*
i is pronounced like *ee* in *feet*
j is pronounced like *y* in *young*
š is pronounced like *sh* in *sheep*
ž is pronounced like *s* in *pleasure*

The Golden Apple

Bride

Gold thread wound out of the sea
Wound round the waist of the first-born
Gold thread wound out of the sea
Wound round the stirrup of the bridesman
Fine thread wound out of the sea
Wound round the standard of the best man
Gold thread wound out of the sea
Wound round the prayers of the husband's brothers
Gold thread wound out of the sea
Wound round the toasting-cup of the bodyguards' leader
Gold thread wound out of the sea
Wound round and round the honour of all the guests

To the Maple Tree

A maple tree went walking
Eyeing all the girls
"Which of all you girls is mine?
Speak up now"
"Maple
I am
But I won't come to you
Until you cut me
A dress of poppy petals
With sleeves of silk"

The Pear Tree

Ivan only has
A small patch of land
But it's good land
Roses and feathergrass
Small pearls and precious stones
In front of his courtyard
A gilded bridge
To his courtyard
A silver gate
In his courtyard
A fine pear tree
As high as the clear sky
As broad as half Sarajevo
Its leaves fall around Belgrade
Its scent spreads to Pešt and Budim

The Golden Apple and the Nine Peahens

Once there was a king, with three sons. Outside his palace there stood a golden apple tree. It bloomed and fruited in a single night, but someone (no one could find out who) stole the fruit. One day the King was talking to his sons: "Where does the fruit from our apple tree go?" The eldest answered "I'll stand guard tonight to see who steals it."

When dark fell, he went off to the apple tree and lay down under it to guard it. However, when the apples were just beginning to ripen, he fell asleep and when he woke up at dawn, there was the tree, stripped. He went to his father and told him what had happened.

Then the second son offered to guard the apple tree. The same thing happened. Now it was the turn of the youngest son to guard the tree. He set his bed up under it and lay down to sleep. Just before midnight, he woke up and looked at the tree. It was just beginning to ripen, the whole courtyard shone with it. At that moment nine golden peahens flew up, eight fell on the tree, the ninth fell into his bed.

When she fell on the bed, she became the most beautiful girl in the whole kingdom. They kissed and cuddled each other until after midnight. Then the girl got up and thanked him for the apples. He asked her to leave him at least one; she left him two, one for him, and one for his father. Then the girl became a peahen again and flew off with the others. At dawn the son got up and took his father both apples. The King was delighted.

Riddles

SUN

One plate serves the whole world.

MOON

A dappled mare jumps over the sea, but doesn't
wet its hooves.

EARTH

Red as blood, black as night
Every man has me to wife.

WIND

I passed through water and was not wet
I passed through fire and was not burnt.

*

I came out on to the silver threshing-floor,
played on a golden pipe; everyone heard me, no
one saw me.

WINTER

No teeth, no hands, but it still bites.

ICE

I gave birth to my mother, and my mother gave birth to me.

SNOW

I flew like an eagle, fell like a king, died like a dog.

SNOW EARTH AND SUN

A white bird flew with no wings, dropped on a dry tree with no branches, a king with no hands killed it, a queen with no teeth ate it.

Angelica the Doorkeeper

The falcon soars
The town's gates are even higher

Angelica's their doorkeeper
She's wound the sun round her head
She's tied the moon round her waist

She's hung herself with stars

Girl

Why are you so smooth-faced
So slender-waisted?
Have you braided the sun's hair
Swept the moon's courtyards clean?

I haven't braided the sun's hair
Or swept the moon's courtyards
I stood outside and watched
Lightning dancing with thunder
Lightning outdanced thunder
By two or three apples
Four oranges

The Dark Country

Once upon a time, there was a king who came with his army to the end of the world, and went into the dark country, where you can't see anything. He left the foals of the mares he had with him on the other side, so the mares would be certain to lead them back.

When they went into the dark country and were moving through it, they kept feeling small stones under their feet. Something called out from the darkness "He who takes some of these stones will regret it, and he who takes none of them will regret it." Some of them thought "Well, if I regret it, why bother?" Some thought "Well, why not take one, at least?"

When they came out of the dark, they saw these were precious stones. Those who took none regretted they hadn't taken any; those who took some regretted they hadn't taken more.

Proverbs

If there were no wind, cobwebs would cover the sky.

*

When it thunders, each man is afraid of himself.

*

Even the sun goes through mud, but it doesn't get dirty.

*

Even water has teeth.

*

When did fog ever uproot a tree-trunk?

To a Child

Daughter-in-law Neda
Buy this child
If you don't want him
We'll take him off
To our country
There in our country
Two suns shining
Two suns shining
Two winds blowing

We need a child
Like a sprig of basil

Angel Children

A man had two children, a son and a daughter. One day he caught a pigeon and gave it to his wife to cook and bring to him while he was working in the fields. His wife prepared lunch and carried it out. On the way she fell, broke the dish and spilt all the food. Her husband was hot-tempered and she didn't dare go to him without food. So she went home quickly, cut off one of her breasts, cooked it and took it to her husband.

When he was eating, the wife asked him how he liked the food. He said he'd never tasted anything sweeter. Then she said "Well, husband, it's my breast you're eating" and told him what she had done. "You see" she said "how sweet human flesh is. Come on, let's shut up our children in a barrel, feed them up, then kill them and eat them." The man agreed, so they caught the children, shut them up in a barrel, and fed them there.

When the day came for them to be killed, the poor children wept and said "St Friday and St Sunday, burst the hoops of our barrel so we can run away from our mother and father." The hoops burst and the children ran off. As they were going they came to a great field where dog-headed men were ploughing and digging. The children helped the dog-heads to dig, and the dog-heads gave them bread so they shouldn't die of hunger.

In the evening, the children pretended to be asleep and the father and mother dog-head talked over how they would make the children into food for the workers next day. The old man said "Woman, put that great cauldron of water on the fire, send them to see if it's boiling and push them in." When dawn broke, the dog-heads went off into the field but the old woman stayed behind to prepare the cauldron for the children.

When it was time, the old woman tried to send the children to see whether the cauldron was boiling, but the children wouldn't go and said "Old woman, we are little and don't know how. Come with us and show us, so we'll know another time." The old woman did as they asked and went with them to the cauldron. As she was leaning over it to see if it was boiling, the children pushed her in and ran off.

When the dog-heads came back, they saw their mother in the cauldron, and at once rushed after the children. They came to a great wood where the children were hidden. Then one shouted "Children, how shall we get to you?" And the children replied "Go home and fetch picks and dig up the wood. You'll get to us that way." The dog-heads went home to fetch picks and the children went out of the wood and came to a great stretch of water. After several days the dog-heads came with picks and dug up the wood, but didn't find the children. They followed after them at once, but the children had already crossed the water and were sitting on the bank.

When the dog-heads saw the children, they began to shout "Children, how shall we get to you?" And the children replied "Hang sacks of stones under your arms and swim out. That's how you'll get to us." The dog-heads did as they said, put sacks of stones under their arms, swam out and were all drowned. The brother and sister came to a spring and wanted to wash and drink there, but something said to them from the spring "Don't touch this water, children, the stars bathe here." They went further on and came to another spring, and again they wanted to wash and drink water, but something said to them from the spring "Don't touch the water, the moon bathes here."

The children went on and came to the spring where the sun bathes and wanted to drink from it and wash in it, but something said to them from the spring "Don't touch this water, children, the sun bathes here." Finally the children came to a fourth spring, where God bathes. Here they drank and washed their faces and sat down to rest. Soon God came out of the spring, blessed the children and turned them into angels.

The Shepherd

The sky is scattered with stars
The field with sheep
There's no shepherd
But Radoje
He's asleep
Silly boy
Janja his sister wakes him
"Radoje get up
Your sheep have got out"
"Let them go, sister
Witches have eaten me up
My mother took out my heart
My aunt held the light"

Curses

May the earth chase you and the sea spit you out!

*

May you be as bent as a sickle in the mountains!

*

May you be as restless as a mill-stone!

*

May you count your teeth on your hand!

Proverbs

Who rails at the stars
Has his teeth fall out.

*

Who weeps for the world
Loses his eyes.

*

Who sleeps with lice
Will be full of fleas.

Riddles

MAN

Earth digging earth.

HEAD

Pot with seven holes
Pour water in and it doesn't run out.

EYES

Two pillars hitting the sky.

*

Two magpies perched on one bone
One can't see the other.

EYESIGHT

I stretched a gold thread through the wide world
and wound it up into a walnut shell.

TEARS

Pearls spilled down a field of men –
They don't stay where they fall.

CORPSE AND BEARERS

Five bodies, four souls, a hundred nails.

Once there was a man and he had a son. This son said one day to his father "Father, what shall we do? I can't live like this; I'm going off into the world to learn a craft. These days, a man who knows even the least craft lives better than any peasant." The father tried for a long time to dissuade him, saying there were worries and hard work in crafts also, and how could he leave his father alone! But when his son would not be dissuaded, he let him go.

So he went off into the world to look for a craft. On his travels he came to a stretch of water, and walking beside it he met a man in green robes. The man asked him where he was going, and he replied "I'm going into the world to find a master-craftsman to teach me a craft." Then the man in green said "I'm a master-craftsman. Come with me." The boy was delighted and went off with him.

As they were walking along by the water, suddenly the master jumped in and began to swim and said to the boy "Come on, jump in, don't be afraid, and learn to swim." And the boy jumped and began to swim alongside the master. When they got to the middle of the water, the master took the child by the scruff of the neck down to the bottom. It was the devil. He took the child off to his palace and handed him over to an old woman to teach him, and then returned to this world.

When the old woman was alone with the child, she said to him "My son, don't think this man is a master like all the other masters. He's the devil. I'm a Christian like you, and he deceived me and brought me down here. Do what I tell you. I'll teach you all his craft, and whenever he comes, and asks you if you've learnt anything, always say 'nothing', if you want to save yourself and go back to the world."

After a while the devil came and asked the child "What have you learnt?" And he answered "Nothing yet." So three years passed, and whenever the master asked the boy what he had learnt, he would always answer that he had learnt nothing. At last the devil asked him once more: "Have you learnt anything at all?" And the boy answered "Nothing, and what I knew before I've forgotten." Then the devil became angry and said to him: "If you haven't learnt anything up to now, you'll never learn anything, so go wherever your eyes lead you and your feet carry you."

The boy, who had mastered the devil's craft very well, jumped into the water at once, swam to the shore, and went off to his father. The father, when he caught sight of him in the distance, ran out to meet him saying "For God's sake, son, where have you been?" And the son answered "I've been learning a craft."

Some time passed. A fair came to a neighbouring village. The son said to his father "Let's go to the fair." "What shall we take when we haven't anything?" "Don't worry about that" answered the son, and they went off to the fair. On the way, the son said to the father "When we get near the fair, I'll turn into a beautiful horse. There won't be another one like me in the whole fair. The whole fair will be amazed. My master will come to buy me and whatever price you ask, he'll pay it. Don't under any circumstances give him the bridle, but when you take the money, slip the bridle off my head and strike the ground with it."

When they got close to the fair, the boy changed into a horse. The old man led the horse through the fair, the whole fair thronged round, no one dared ask how much such a beautiful horse would be. The master came. He'd turned himself into a Turk, wound a turban round his head, let his robes flow down onto the ground. He came up to the father and said "I'll buy that horse. How much do you want for it?" Whatever the old man asked, the Turk pulled out of his money-bag without protest. When the old man had taken the money, he took the bridle off the horse, and hit it on the ground. Horse and merchant vanished. The man went home and there was his son, as if nothing had happened.

A while later, there was another fair and the son again said to his father "Come on, father, let's go to the fair." The father didn't say anything this time, but went off at once. When they were near the fair, the son said "I'll turn myself into merchandise – a tent full of goods. The whole fair will be astonished at their beauty and rich- ness. No one will be able to buy it, but my master will come and pay you whatever price you ask. Don't, what- ever you do, give him the keys, but when you take the money throw the keys on the ground."

He turned into merchandise. The whole fair was amazed. The Turk came along again. "How much?" he asked. Whatever the old man asked, he paid. When the old man got all the money, he threw the keys on the ground. Merchandise and Turk disappeared; the merchandise became a dove and the Turk a hawk chasing the dove. The Emperor's daughter came out of her palace and watched them. Suddenly, the dove dived straight onto the girl's hand and became a ring. Then the hawk fell to the ground and became a man and went off to the Emperor and offered to serve him; he'd serve him three years, and ask nothing in return, nothing at all, no food, no drink, no clothes, but just that ring from the Princess's hand.

The Emperor accepted him and promised that he'd give him the ring. So he served his three years, and the girl wore the ring, and was very happy, since by day it was a ring but by night became a handsome young man who said to her "When the time comes for them to take me from you, don't give me into anyone's hand, but throw me to the ground."

When three years had passed, the Emperor came to his daughter, and begged her to give him the ring. She pretended to be angry and threw the ring onto the floor. The ring broke, and fine cornmeal spilt from it. One grain rolled away under the Emperor's boot. At that the Emperor's servant became a sparrow and began to peck up the corn frantically. When he'd pecked up all the corn, he hopped across the floor to peck up that last grain under the Emperor's boot. The grain became a cat and grabbed the sparrow by the neck.

To a Schoolboy

Ploughman ploughing a level field
His plough a magic tree
An oleaster tree

Ploughing a level field
His ploughshare a grey dove
His goad a sprig of basil
His oxen two stags

Instead of wheat
He's sowing small pearls
Ploughing with a magic feather
A peacock feather

Proverbs

A man is bound by his word
An ox by his horns.

*

Tree leans on tree
Man on man.

*

Even when a man falls
He's resting.

*

When his house burns
A man can at least warm himself.

*

A threshold is the highest mountain.

*

A man learns while he's alive
He still dies a fool.

Riddles

WALNUT

I threw a stick sky-high and look! a circle of dancing girls fell down.

WATERMELON

With an iron key
I open a green fortress
And drive out the black cattle.

PLUM

A dun cow fell from heaven, split her belly, kept her calf.

ACORN

Wood rides a wood horse; wood cap, scar on its head.

The Girl Faster than a Horse

Once there was a girl who wasn't born to a father and mother, but was made by spirits from snow they took from the bottomless pit facing the sun of Elijah. The wind brought her to life, the dew suckled her, the forest clothed her with leaves and the meadow decked her out with flowers. She was whiter than snow, redder than roses, more shining than the sun, no one was ever born on earth like her, nor ever will be.

She let it be known that on a certain day in a certain place there would be a race, and whichever young man on horseback could outrun her, she would be his. In a few days all the world knew, and thousands of suitors came on horses, and it was impossible to say who was the best. The son of the King himself came to the race. The girl stood at the mark and all the suitors lined up on their horses. She didn't have a horse, she was on foot. She said "I have put a golden apple over there; he who gets to it first and takes it, I'll be his, but if I get to it first, you'll all fall dead where you are, so beware!"

The horsemen looked at each other, each hoping he'd win the girl, and they said to each other "We know for sure she won't outrun all of us on foot. One of us is bound to win. Whoever it is, God give him luck!"

The girl clapped her hands, and they all set off immediately. When they were half way the girl was far out in front – she had spread little wings out under her arms. Then they all upbraided each other, and whipped and spurred their horses and caught the girl up. When she saw this, she pulled a hair out of her head and threw it down, and it grew up at once into a terrible forest, so the suitors didn't know where they were or where to go. She got well ahead but they spurred their horses and caught her up.

Again when the girl saw the forest hadn't worked, she let fall a tear – and terrible rivers gushed out and nearly drowned them all. After that, no one went on with the chase except the King's son. He swam out on his horse after her, but when he saw the girl had outrun him he called her three times in God's name to stop. She stopped where she was. He seized her, threw her onto his horse behind him, swam to dry land, and set off home over the mountain. When he came to the top of the mountain, he looked round.

The girl was gone.

Proverbs

Eyes are water.

*

The belly has no window.

*

The soul has one door.

*

What use are pearls if they choke me?

*

If I were to touch a green pine, even the green
pine would wither.

Judge Girl Grass

A girl fell asleep in the grass
The grass stole the pink of the girl's skin
The girl took the green from the grass
The girl went to court
"Grass
Give me back the pink of my skin"
The grass answered
"I'll give it you back
When you give back my green"
How could they go on?
Before the judge, they swore to be sisters

Riddles

COMB

One dead pulls a hundred live from a mountain.

NEEDLE

I am young and slender
When I travel I have a tail
The further I go
The less there is of my tail
I lose it as I go
And come home tailless.

TROUSERS

I jumped into a pit
And came out at two gates.

Proverbs

His mind's wandering through the world, but
the axe is at his neck.

*

A too cunning man jumps over his luck.

*

You can't feed the wolves and keep all the sheep.

*

For one man, lead will float, for another a straw
will sink.

*

He hides it as a snake hides its feet.

The Witch

A man had two servants, who worked together and ate the same food, but one was withered and weak and the other was healthy. How could this be? Whenever he asked whether the man was in pain, he always said no. The master's wife, though, was a witch. Almost every evening when the servant lay down to sleep, she took some ointment, anointed him, and he became a horse. Then she'd bridle him, mount him and ride him to Klek or Velebit or Pješevica all night long.

When she'd had her fill of dancing and riding, she'd come back, unharness him, and he'd become a man again. When he'd had enough of this, the servant told the master everything. "If only you could see, master, how lovely it is there – there's a threshing floor made only of bronze and they gather there, all so beautifully dressed you can't say which is most beautiful. When they've all gathered there, they dance and they tie us up to beams of silver and in the mangers there are rings of gold, but in spite of all that they don't give us anything to eat." And the master said "See if you can't find out where she gets the ointment from. Hide it and she won't be able to go any more."

So the servant watched, caught her out, and one day when they came home, went to the cupboard where the ointment was and hid it. When she fell asleep, he anointed her and she turned into a fine mare, you couldn't find a better anywhere. He went first to a smith and had her well-shod, and then rode her to all the places she had ridden him. When he had ridden round everywhere with her, he came back home, took off the bridle, and she became a woman again and lay down to sleep.

Dawn came; the master and servant got up, but the wife wouldn't. When her husband came to her and asked her why she wouldn't, she said "Leave me alone, I beg you as a brother. I'm in a bad way." "Why?" he said. "Look here" she said and pointed to her hands and feet. She was still shod. The man saw at once what was up, went off and brought the smith, who took off the shoes. After that the wife was never able to ride to the bronze threshing floor again.

Proverbs

Watch out for secret coals.

*

When your enemy is an ant, fear him like a lion.

*

Sit crooked, but talk straight.

*

You can't block out the sun with your hand.

Riddles

TINDER-BOX

Two that were dead fought
A third was born, alive.

FIRE

Dragon's nest in the middle of the house.

COAL

Red hen with fire on her head.

SPECTACLES

One head, four eyes
Two in a cave
Two riding a horse.

PIPE

Fire burning on the snake's head
The pasha kissing her tail.

Nothing Can Be Hidden

Two lovers kissed in a meadow
They thought no one saw them
The green meadow saw them
Told the white flock
The flock told its shepherd
The shepherd told a traveller
The traveller told a ferryman
The ferryman told his walnut boat
The boat told the cold water
The water told the girl's mother
The girl was furious

"Meadow, may you never be green!
White flock, may wolves eat you!
Shepherd, may the Turks hack you down!
Traveller, may your legs rot!
Ferryman, may water carry you off!
Ferry-boat, burn! Water, dry up!"

The Poplar's Complaint

Poplar
Why did you cry out last night?
Were you drowning?
Were you on fire?
Was the army looting you?
Were sheep trampling you?
Were girls pulling you apart?

I wasn't drowning
I wasn't on fire
The army wasn't looting me
The sheep weren't trampling me
It was the girls pulling me apart
Get them married off
Or don't plant poplars

Lovers' Parting

Two flowers grew in a garden
Blue hyacinth, red rose
The hyacinth went away
The rose was left alone
The hyacinth sent a message
"How are you, my darling,
Alone in the garden?"
The rose replied
"If the sky were a piece of paper
The forest pens
The sea black ink
If I were to write for three years
I could not write out my pain"

Against Sleeplessness

The wind blows over high forests, broad fields, great
waters, over full ears of barley, thin hemp, strong-
rooted maize, over fruitful trees and grape-heavy vines,
the wind blows over foxes, wolves, hares, bears, stags,
deer, sheep, goats, horses, cattle, hens, doves, titmice,
quails, cuckoos, partridges, magpies, ravens, jackdaws,
nightingales, falcons . . . the wind blows over everything
and everyone to come here and blow Milan sweet sleep.

Spell Against Scab

St Wednesday is marrying off her son
St Friday is giving her daughter away
They've invited everyone
Even Plague, even Smallpox.
They haven't invited Scab, though
Scab is angry
Don't be angry
Dry up
Like sheep's wool on a fence

So Milan may be
Healthy as a cherry tree
Light as a feather
So Milan may sleep
Like a lamb in spring grass

There were nine brothers, all nine went off to the war, all nine were killed with guns, all nine were cut down with sabres, all nine were pierced with spikes.

Of that nine eight came back, of that eight seven, of that seven six, of that six five, of that five four, of that four three, of that three two, of that two one, of that one not one.

Against Eye-Ache

My eyes are hurting, and won't stop.

Two leaves flew down and said "We'll take the shadow your eyes have, and carry it high up under our wings and put it under the clouds and pick two stars and put them on your eyes."

A man had a baby son. He didn't have anyone to baptize the child, so he set off to find a godmother. On the way, a dragon met him, and asked to be the baby's godmother. The man gave her the child and she christened it. When they parted, the dragon invited the baby's mother to visit her.

Next day the mother went to visit her, but when she sat down in the first room she saw a shovel and a broom fighting; when she went into a second room, there were human hands; when she sat down in a third room, there were human feet; when she sat down in the fourth room there was human flesh; when she sat down in the fifth room there was blood, and when she sat down in the sixth room, there was the dragon taking off her head, searching it for fleas, and putting a horse's head on instead.

When she saw the mother, she threw off the horse's head and put on her own. Then the dragon brought food to her and said "Eat, sister, eat." "How can I eat? When I went into the first room a shovel and broom were fighting." "Eat, sister, eat. Those are my servants, they fight over who should sweep the room." "How can I eat, sister, when I sat in the second and third rooms and there were human hands and feet?" "Eat, sister, eat, that is my food." "How can I eat, sister, when I sat in the fourth room and there was human flesh?" "Eat, dear sister, eat, that is my bread." "How can I eat, sister, when I sat in the fifth room, and there was only blood?" "Eat, sister, eat, that is the wine I drink." "How can I eat when I saw you take off your head and search it for fleas and put on a horse's head?"

When she heard that, the dragon gobbled up both her and her child. The man came and asked "Sister, where are my wife and child?" "Brother, they had lunch and went off, and I haven't seen them since." The father went off to search for them, and he searched, but never found them.

How Raki Came to Be

When God chased the first man out of paradise
He filled him with pain
Man couldn't bear that pain
Gave it to the earth
Earth couldn't bear that pain
Gave it to the forest
The forest went white
Gave it to rock
Rock melted
Gave it back to man
Man would have gone mad
If it wasn't for the Devil
He built a building on four beams
Left gates on all sides
Turned water into raki there
And sold it

Riddles

POT

It's made of the same thing as Adam, it's tormented like Adam; when it dies, though, there's no soul for God, no bones for the earth.

POT AND SPOON

Earth weeps, the forest tickles it.

SPOON

A horse with its pack goes into a house and comes out of it, but its tail never goes in.

CAULDRON

Black dog hanging from the sky.

THE VINE AND THE WINE

The father in the cradle, the son courting.

CELLAR

I'm darkest when it's light; I'm hottest when it's cold; I'm coldest when it's warm.

To a Hero

A leaf of an orange tree
Fell into a hero's cup
If the leaf had known
It was a hero's cup
It would have curled upwards
And drunk it dry

Proverbs

He gets in your eyes like sweat.

*

Time hangs heavy on him, so he's counting the
goats' names.

*

They won't do anything to him, just hang him a
little and let him go.

*

A wolf pays with his skin.

*

Measure a wolf's tail when he's dead.

*

Even his tail is a burden to a tired fox.

*

A lot of dogs can eat a wolf.

How the Mole Came to Be

A peasant wanted to steal his neighbour's field. He buried his son in the ground, after telling him what to say to any question he was asked. The magistrates came to the field with the defendant, and the man who wanted to seize the other's property said: "Black earth, speak, whose are you?" "I am yours, I am yours" they heard a child's voice cry from the earth.

The real owner, when he heard that, was afraid and the magistrates decided in favour of the unjust man. When they had all gone, the father took a spade and hurried to dig his child out. The child wasn't there! The father called him, and the child replied, but from further and further away. He had become a mole.

Aga Asan-Aga

Aga Asan-Aga was gathering herbs
In Mostar
In the middle of Sarajevo
A Rumanian saw him
Near Vienna
He aimed his gun at Belgrade
Hit him where it hurts
Below the knee between both eyes
Aga Asan-Aga fell dead
He fell dead
He came home safe and sound

Shut Up, Damn You!

They say that the Turkish Sultan feeds and clothes idlers. First of all, however, they are examined to see if they're real idlers, or not.

Two men came to be taken on as idlers. They were sat on a rush-mat. The mat was set on fire. One said "Get up! Let's get out of here! We'll burn to death!" The other answered "Shut up, damn you! How can you be bothered to speak?"

Give Me The Gallows When You Hang Me

A man was condemned to death. He asked someone to tell him what "the gallows" were, and what they were made of. When they brought him to the gallows, he asked the judge "Please, sir, when you hang me, give me these gallows to take home to my good wife Georgia — she's left at home with three children without a stick of firewood." "All right" replied the judge. Then the man said: "How would it be, sir, if you made them a bit lower . . . I won't be in any state to carry them if you don't help me."

Curses

God give you a heart of snow and feet of tallow,
so in winter you can't warm yourself by the fire
and in summer you can't go into the sun!

*

God give you a thousand dogs, all dumb, so you
have to run round the house and bark yourself.

*

God make you black as a pot, thin as a thread —
may you pass through the stem of a pipe and sit
cross-legged in its bowl.

*

God give you a gold coin weighing a ton, so you
can't carry it or spend it, but have to sit beside it,
begging.

Riddles

BREAD

A white bull goes into the basket with no skin
and comes out with one.

TURNIP

It's white, but isn't cheese.
It has a tail, but isn't a mouse.
It licks salt, but isn't an ox.

MARROW

I sowed little cakes
Cords grew
I harvested little logs.

COCK

It came out of a white stone. It has a dress not
made by hands. At its voice the dead awake.
After death, they baptize it.

EGG

In one room both bone and flesh grow.

DUCK

My breast is a boat
The oars are my feet
My hands are between my eyes.

DOG

Two shine, four stretch, one thinks about lying down.

BAGPIPES

A dead billy-goat's voice ringing through the whole village.

*

Killed, flayed, goes home singing.

GUSLE

Wooden belly. Leather back. Speaks with hairs.

Spell Against Jaundice

Yellow cock
Beat your yellow wings three times
Over a yellow hen
A yellow hen in a yellow year
In a yellow month
In a yellow week
On a yellow day
Laid a yellow egg
In yellow hay
Let the yellow hay stay
And the yellow fever leave our Milan.

Yellow bitch
Whelp your yellow pup
On a yellow day
In a yellow week
In a yellow month
In a yellow year
In a yellow wood
Let the yellow wood stay
And the yellow fever leave our Milan.

Yellow cow calve a yellow calf
On a yellow day
In a yellow week
In a yellow month
In a yellow year
In a yellow field

Let the yellow field stay
And the yellow fever leave our Milan.
Hoooh!

Yellow candle
Of yellow wax
Burn in a yellow room
Burn out
Be as if you had never been
Together with our Milan's yellow fever.

Stop – no further!
This is not your place!
Go into the deep sea
Into the high hills . . .

Get up, get out, witches and winds, you've come to eat up Milan's heart and head, but Dora is a wise-woman and is with him, and sends you out into the forest to count the leaves, to the sea to measure the sand, into the world to count all the paths, and when you come back you won't be able to do anything to him. Dora the wise-woman has blown you away with her breath, swept you away with her hand, scattered you with herbs. Look – life and health are upon our Milan.

Riddles

BEES AND THE BEEHIVE

I let out the sheep and milked the sheepfold.

SILKWORM

A bride lording it in a green meadow; she pecks up green and sicks up gold.

HOUSE

A mare in the middle of the field, live foals jump out of her.

WINDOW

Our granny has glass eyes.

PADLOCK

Black louse guards the house.

Basil and Dew

The basil complained
"Quiet dew, why don't you fall on me?"
"I did for two mornings
But today I'm distracted
I've been watching
A vila quarrelling with an eagle
Around that green mountain"
The vila cried "This mountain's mine"
The eagle cried "No, it's mine"
So the vila broke the eagle's wings
Which set the eaglets crying
In anger and fear
But a swallow comforted them
"Eaglets, don't be sad
I'll take you to India
Where sweet grass grows
High as a horse's knee
And clover grass grows
High as a horse's shoulder
And the sun never sets"
And the eaglets heard and were comforted

vila: a mountain-spirit

The Peacock Finds Food

The peacock finds food, the grass grows
The wood is green
Branch meets with leaf
But I have no one
My lover is away
In another country
I send a message
"Come, my darling
A rose is blooming in my garden
I can't pick it
On the rose
A nightingale's singing
I can't hear it"
"I can't come, my darling
For another year
The empty roads are closed
From Rumelija
Sender-Bey has closed them
We are dying
From sorrow"

The Animals' Language

A man had a shepherd who had served him for many years. One day, when he was following the sheep, he heard a squealing from the wood and did not know what it was. He went towards it and saw a fire and a snake in the fire. "Shepherd, for God's sake, get me out of this fire" the snake cried. The shepherd reached out his stick across the fire, and the snake crawled along it, up his arm, and curled round his neck.

When the shepherd saw that, he said "What is this? What a misfortune! I've saved you and destroyed myself." The snake said "Don't be afraid, but take me home to my father. My father is king of the snakes." The shepherd began to plead that he couldn't leave the sheep, but the snake said to him "Don't worry about the sheep at all, nothing will happen to them; just come quickly with me." So the shepherd went with the snake through the wood and came at last to a gate made entirely of snakes.

When they got there, the snake round his neck whistled, and the other snakes at once unwound themselves. Then the snake said to the shepherd "When we come to the court of my father, he will give you whatever you ask – silver, gold, anything – but don't ask for that, ask for the animals' language. He'll hesitate a long time, but will give it to you in the end."

They came to his father's court; seeing his son, the father wept and asked him "Where have you been?" and the snake told him everything and how the shepherd had saved him. Then the King of the snakes said to the shepherd "What would you like me to give you for saving my son?" The shepherd answered: "I don't want anything – except the animals' language." The King said "That isn't for you – if I gave it to you and you told anyone else, you'd die at once. Ask for something else, anything . . ." But the shepherd said "If you want to give me something, give me the animals' language . . . If you won't give me that, goodbye, I don't need anything else." And he made as if to go.

Then the King called him back, saying "Stop, come here, if that's what you really want . . . Open your mouth." The shepherd opened his mouth, and the King Snake spat into it. "Now you spit into my mouth." The shepherd spat into his mouth and then the King Snake spat again into the shepherd's mouth. And they spat three times into each other's mouth, and then the King Snake said "Now you have the animals' language. Go with God, but don't whatever you do tell anyone, for if you do you'll die at once." The shepherd went through the wood, and as he went he heard and understood all that the birds and the grass and everything else in the world was saying.

Sisters that had no Brother

Two sisters had no brother
So they wove him of white silk
And red silk
His waist was of box-wood
His black eyes were two jewels
His eyebrows sea-leeches
His teeth two rows of pearls
They gave him honey and sugar
"Speak to us"

Jovo and Ana

Jovo was scything the meadow
Ana was bleaching her linen on the meadow
She stretched it out on the grass
And flattened his grass
Jovo said
"Ana
Don't flatten my grass
You can't straighten it again
If I could forgive you that
I wouldn't forgive you
Touching my heart
If you were water I'd drink you
If you were a flower I'd wear you
If you were a fir tree I'd break your branches
And shade my face from the sun
If you were the sun I'd be proud of you
If you were dew I'd wash my face in you
And rest in the wet grass"
Ana ran from him through the wood
The grass was lush and high
Ana has three layers of skirt
Long skirts high grass
Ana can't get away from him
Jovo caught her up in the meadow
Took her to his white house
Took her to be his true love

Riddles

CUSHION

He goes to wash, leaves his belly at home.

SCALES

His mind's in his tail.

SAW

Wooden body, iron teeth, gnaws through stone.

GUN

Hangs on a nail, thinks evil.

A Tall Story

A father sent his son off to grind corn. He told him not to grind it in any mill where he found a bald miller. The first mill the son came to he found a bald man sitting there. "God bless, Baldy." "God bless you, son." "Could I grind some wheat here?" "Of course you can. Mine will soon be ground and then you can grind as much as you want."

The boy, however, remembered what his father had said, left, and walked up-stream to another mill. But the bald man had run to the mill by another path, and put out some corn there. When the boy came to this mill and saw the bald man was there too, he went on to a third; the same thing happened; he went on to a fourth; the same thing happened again. The boy was fed up and thought: there's probably a bald man in every mill. So he took the bag of corn off his back and stopped to grind it with the bald man.

When the bald man's corn was ground and the child had put his in to grind, the bald man said "Come on, boy, let's make a loaf from your flour." The child still remembered what his father had said – that he shouldn't grind where there was a bald man, but now he thought: Well, since I'm here, I might as well stay. So he said to the bald man "Come on, then." The bald man got up and shook the child's flour into the flour-bin and told the child to bring water in handfuls. The child brought water, the bald man mixed the water in gradually, little by little as all the corn was ground. Then the bald man mixed the flour, made a large loaf, blew up a fire and put it in to bake.

When the loaf was baked they took it off the fire and leant it against the wall. Then the bald man said to the boy "If we divide this loaf, you know, there won't be much for either of us. Come on, let's tell tall stories to each other, and the one who tells the tallest story gets the loaf." The boy thought to himself: There's nothing for it, and said "Let's go. Your turn first."

The bald man began to tell a few lies, here and there, and when he'd told his tallest stories and was tired the boy said "Well, Baldy, you're not much good, are you? I'll tell you a really true story. When I was an old man in my youth, we had a lot of beehives and I'd count them every morning, and I'd count all the bees, but couldn't count the hives. One morning I counted the bees, the best bee wasn't there; so, in a flash, I saddled a cockerel and rode off to look for it. I tracked it to the sea, but it had gone over it, so I followed its track. When I'd crossed the sea, I saw a man had yoked my bee to a plough and was ploughing for millet. I shouted at him 'That's my bee. Where did you get my bee from?' And he answered 'If it's your bee, take it.' And he gave me the bee and a full bag of millet he'd just ploughed. I shouldered the bag of millet, put the saddle from the cock on to the bee, mounted the bee, and led the cock on a bridle to rest it. When we were over the sea, one of the straps of the bag burst, and all the millet fell out into the sea.

"When I had crossed the sea night fell so I got off the bee, and left him free to graze, tied up the cock by me, gave him some hay and lay down to sleep. When in the morning I got up, wolves had come and killed and eaten my bee; honey was in the valley ankle-high, and in the hills knee-high. Then I started to think what I could collect the honey in. I remembered I had a little axe, so I took it and went into the wood to catch some animals to make into a bag. Two deer came jumping towards me on one leg. I swung the axe, broke their one leg, seized them, flayed them into three bags, and collected all the honey into them, loaded it onto the cock, and took it all home.

"When I got home, my father had just been born, so they sent me to God to get some holy water. How on earth would I get up to heaven, I wondered to myself. Then I remembered that millet spilt into the sea. When I got there it had fallen on a damp place and grown up to heaven – so let's go to heaven then. When I got to the top, the millet was ripe, God had harvested it and made bread from it, had crumbled it into hot milk and was eating it. I said 'God bless, God' and he said 'God bless' and gave me the water.

"When I came back, it had unfortunately been raining – the sea had come up and flooded everywhere and swept everything away. How in heaven am I going to get back to earth, I thought. Then I remembered I had long hair; when I stand, it reaches the ground, when I sit, it reaches my ears, so I took a knife and cut it off, hair by hair, and tied it together. When dark fell, I tied a knot in the hair and spent the night there. What would I do without fire though? I had a flint and no wood! Suddenly I remembered I had a needle in my sheepskin coat so I got it out, pulled it to pieces, made a fire, warmed myself nicely, then lay down by the fire to sleep.

"While I slept, though, a spark jumped out of the fire and burnt the hair up, and I fell headlong onto the earth and stuck in it up to my waist. I twisted and turned to try and pull myself out, but when I saw it wouldn't work, I ran off home and got a spade and dug myself out and took the water home.

"When I came home, reapers were reaping in the field. There was a real heat up, dear God, the reapers might burn up in it. So I called out 'Why don't you go and get that mare of ours that's two days long and broad as noon, with willows growing out of her shoulders, she'll give you cool shade!' My father ran off in a flash, got the mare, and the reapers began to reap happily in the shade. I took a bucket and went off to fetch water.

"When I got there, the water was frozen, so I took off my head, broke the ice with it and took some water. When I brought the water to the reapers, they shouted 'Where's your head?' I felt with my hands, my head wasn't there, I'd forgotten it by the water. I raced back – and a fox was eating my brain; I crept up, got close and gave the fox a good kick. She was so scared she dropped her accounts book. When I opened it there was written – a loaf for me, a fig for Baldy." Then the boy got up, took the loaf, and Baldy was left gazing after him.

The Tallest of Tall Stories

A ship sailed over the cliffs
A knight danced his horse over the sea
Two roast hares are running through the field
Chased by two flayed hounds
Two blind huntsmen are waiting for them
Two dead heroes are drinking wine
Serving it
Is a girl without arms

The Death of the Kettle

A peasant thought how he could trick a money-lender who had done him down. One day he went to the money-lender and asked him "Sir, please lend me your raki kettle. I'll bring it back in a week, and pay you a shilling for it." The money-lender was tempted and lent him the kettle.

The peasant returned on the seventh day and brought him a very small raki kettle saying "Do you know what, sir?" "What?" asked the money-lender. "Your cauldron was pregnant, and I've brought you its child, since it came to me pregnant and I don't want to keep what is yours."

"Bravo," said the money-lender, "one can see you are an honest man. Thank you!" "Please sir," added the peasant, "let the kettle stay with me a few days longer. I can't send it back now, it's still sick." "Fine" said the money-lender.

After about ten days, the peasant came running, and said "Sir, something dreadful's happened!" "What?" asked the money-lender. "The kettle's dead." "What the hell do you mean?" shouted the money-lender. "How can a kettle die?" "Well," said the peasant, "anything that can have young can die, can't it?"

And so when the money-lender took the peasant to court, the peasant won the case and took the big kettle for the little one.

Proverbs

A lie has short legs.

*

The devil rides on a man who lies.

*

You need a lot of spades to bury truth.

Your Moon is Bigger than Ours

A man went to his blood-brother's name-day the fifth day after the new moon, and stayed several days. One evening after supper they went out and sat in front of the house. The moon was shining bright as day.

The man saw the moon was much bigger than when he left home and said to his blood-brother "Good God! How much bigger your moon is here than ours at home!" "What do you expect?" he answered. "Of course it's bigger and rounder – we fatten it up every day like a pig before slaughter with cheese and hot wine. When we haven't either we give it bread and buttermilk."

Riddles

BRIDGE OVER WATER

God's creation, man's making, a saddled serpent.

BOAT

The dead carries the living over a field of unrest.

*

I sat on the devil and went off without trace.

A BOAT ON THE WATER

A headless horse, a grassless path.

A SHIP ON THE SEA

A swan flew over the shifting field, and came flying home without wings.

The Sailor and the Girl

To shore!
To shore!
"I can't go
My boat has no oars!"
"Take my white arms"
"I can't go
My ship has no sails"
"Take my white skirt"

Proverbs

Get your moustaches together, you're going on a
journey.

*

Have you taken the dew off your heart?

*

I'll hit you so one ear sings and the other weeps.

*

Hold on to the wind with your teeth.

A Beautiful Girl

A beautiful girl was walking
In front of Jovo's house
His mother came out and said
"Stop walking in front of my house!
Go away!
Stop tempting my son!
I'll fence him round
With wood and stones and pine-trunks"
"Do what you like, Mother
I'll just turn into a swallow
Fly over the wood and stones and pine-trunks
And kiss him"

Proverbs

Don't meddle with muck or the pigs will eat you.

*

He who listens to everyone does wrong, he who listens to no one does worse.

*

Even crows lay eggs for a lucky man.

*

If you put him on a wound, it would heal.

*

God has woollen feet, but iron hands.

Riddles

CANDLE

A cat sits on a shelf
In a yellow frame
Knows her own end
Eats her own flesh.

ICON LAMP

A yellow kitten weeps before God.

PIT

The more I chop you up, the bigger you get.

THE SOUND OF A BELL

I shake a tree here, but the fruit falls half-an-
hour away.

The Angel and the Man's Soul

The plague was raging. A man was trying to escape. On the way he overtook an angel who said he was running away also. They went together. When they came to an oak tree, they sat down to rest. The angel took the man's soul, and left his dead body behind.

The angel went on with the man's soul. A little further on, the man's soul cried out "Hey, I've left my shoes under the oak tree." The angel agreed to wait as he went back. He wasn't away long, but came running and shouting "Someone else has got my shoes on! He's under the oak tree, black with flies." "That's you" said the angel. "While we were under the oak tree, you died."

The Drowned Girl

Why does the Morava flow darkly?
Are soldiers sailing away?
Are viziers watering their horses?
Are girls washing linen?
No soldiers are sailing away
No viziers watering horses
No girls washing linen
Two girls were bathing
Alivera and Todora
Todora was drowned
Alivera swam to safety
Todora said
"Alivera
Don't tell my mother
Todora's been drowned
Tell her
She's got married
Two stones were her bridesmen
Two willows – her sisters-in-law
Fine sand – her wedding guests
Her love – cold stone"

BIBLIOGRAPHY

V. Čajkanović, *Srpske narodne pripovetke*, 1927

T. R. Đorđević, *Srpske narodne igre*, 1907

T. R. Đorđević, *Zle oči u verovanju Južnih Slovena*, 1938

V. Đurić, *Narodne lirske pesme*, 1953

V. M. Jovanović, *Srpska narodna pripovetka*, 1932

V. M. Jovanović, *Srpske narodne pesme*, 1937

Vuk Stef. Karadžić, *Srpske narodne pjesme* (I), 1932

Vuk Stef. Karadžić, *Srpske narodne poslovice*, 1933

Vuk Stef. Karadžić, *Srpske narodne pjesme* (V), 1935

Vuk Stef. Karadžić, *Srpske narodne pripovetke*, 1935

M. Đ. Milićević, *Život Srba seljaka*, 1894

Vuk Vrčević, *Narodne basne*, Dubrovnik, 1888

Stojan Novaković, *Srpske narodne zagonetke*, 1877

J. Miodragović, *Narodna pedagogija*, 1914

J. M. Prodanović, *Ženske narodne pesme*, 1925

J. M. Prodanović, *Antologija narodnih pripovedaka*, 1951

This list includes only those collections from which Vasko Popa took items for his anthology. All titles were published in Belgrade, except that by Vrčević.

Serbo-Croat Poetry in translation from Anvil

IVAN V. LALIĆ
Translated by Francis R. Jones

A Rusty Needle

The Passionate Measure

Fading Contact

'Poem after poem ignites in a virtuoso display of metaphor and image'

GERARD SMITH, *Irish Times*

VASKO POPA
Collected Poems

Translated by Anne Pennington
Revised and expanded by Francis R. Jones
With an introduction by Ted Hughes

'Popa's imaginative journey resembles a Universe passing through a Universe. It has been one of the most exciting things in modern poetry, to watch this journey being made.'

TED HUGHES

'What makes these sequences so compelling is the sense that the ultimate riddle with which they are concerned is the riddle of life itself'

DENNIS O'DRISCOLL, *The Times Literary Supplement*

MAK DIZDAR

Stone Sleeper

Translated by Francis R. Jones
with an afterword by Rusmir Mahmutćehajić

Inspired by medieval tombstones and their inscriptions in his native Bosnia, Mak Dizdar's arresting poems express a personal yet universal vision of life and death that owes much to the Gnostic traditions, both Christian and Muslim, which depict life as a passage between 'tomb and stars'. His poetry is (perhaps surprisingly for its time, and in view of the writer's previous impeccably orthodox Communist history) untainted by dogma, religious or political.

Mehmedalija 'Mak' Dizdar (1917–1971) was one of the finest Yugoslav poets of the last century. Rusmir Mahmutćehajić, a leading Bosnian intellectual who is both a physicist and a student of the phenomenology of the sacred, contributes an extended discussion of the poems and their religious and historical background.